OUR
GLORIOUS
FUTURE

THE INTERPRETATION OF

"Light on the Path"

Contents: Self-Conquest; The Disciple; "Attend
You Unto Them"; The Masters; Sight, Hearing;
Speech; Stability; The Transmutation of Desire;
Work and Effort; Separateness; Sensation; The
Retreat; The Advance; The Blooming of the
Flower; Contemplation; The Study of Mankind;
The Study of the Self; The Logos; The Gifts of
the Disciple; The Victory; "I and My Father"

Mabel Collins

ISBN 1-56459-503-X

CONTENTS

PART I

SELF-CONQUEST

CHAPTER I

THE DISCIPLE

"These rules are written for all disciples."

THESE words meant only a few, in the long, slow development during the periods of past history ; and those would have been advanced Yogins.

But now is the turn of the wheel of evolution.

Now [1] they are crowding up from right and left, from north, south, east, and west, hosts of disciples, followers of the Christ, brought into a state of consciousness by the hotbed of War, ready for sacrifice, eager to learn. Men on the battlefield, disciplined to the giving of their lives without grudge, those in the desolated homes at home, praying for strength to learn the lesson set them, rise above the purple pall of grief which is being drawn over the fighting countries, and pass

[1] Written 1917.

into the rose-colour of rebirth and beyond that to the glory ; and all who are so aspiring and so rising enter into the state of the disciple. They crowd the place where these sacred words are written on the wall for all time. They are of all races, all nations, many, many more of some races and of some nations than of others by reason of the order of national development.

It is glorious to see them entering in, with bleeding hearts and streaming eyes, footsore, weary, and sad, but eager for the truth, and ready at rebirth to cast all sadness away. It falls from them like a cloak discarded, and the radiant, ready spirit emerges, ready to kneel at the feet of the Christ, the Master of the Eon, almost strong enough to stand in His presence. Wherever He goes, on the battlefield, in the trenches, in the broken and desolate homes, the newly born, the neophytes, the disciples, awakened by horror and grief, crowd round Him, eager to learn. For they *must* learn—they know this—no lesser thing can satisfy them, no lesser state than that of the disciple can enable them to bear the pain or endure the losses laid on them. And thus the lilies bloom, and the flowers grow, springing from the grief and pain which changes men's hearts and alters all their thoughts and hopes. And the Christ smiles upon all, whispering a sacred word to each, and draws them after Him to swell the ever-increasing upward-going crowd of pilgrims. The Russian peasant mother, devout and faithful, finds her strong son, who went so stern and fierce into the battle, purified and chastened by death from hunger in an enemy prison, reborn as a little child, and as a little child she leads him in the ethereal world as she led him in the physical; learning to stand in the blood of her own heart, because he must be helped. For the disciples of the Christ follow Him in ceaseless labours of love. The quiet, gentle father and mother in a beautiful English home, whose one beloved son has died on the field of glory, enter into such new thoughts and feelings as no length of their chosen, peaceful life could have given them. They know now that there is something beyond it, an inexorable stern force which drags men into conflict and causes them to suffer and die in the gladness of youth; and knowing that, the desire to learn its nature arises within them and they become disciples. For that is the one and only key which opens that door, the desire to know the truth, the willingness to learn.

And the Master—our Great and Good Shepherd—the one Master of all disciples of to-day, smiles on the new flock that crowds around Him, and carries the most feeble and weary, leading them all into the place of learning, where teachers await them and guides are ready to lead them to those they have loved, and fancied they had lost. It is the disciple's desire to learn which draws and commands the teachers and the guides. "Ask, and ye shall have; knock, and it shall be opened to you," said the Christ, and He says it now; for that is a law of life. Who so desires to learn is taught. Perhaps life itself, the great universal teacher, gives him his first lesson, by changing into its other aspect of death, and taking from him his beloved one. If from that dread experience he rises demanding to be taught what is the meaning of it, teachers and guides will come to him; *for he is a disciple.* Intensity of suffering raises men to the point attained by the Yogin by training and effort; sometimes it brings instant illumination. And thus this bitter year in which I am writing is bringing new flocks to the Good Shepherd and raising high hopes among the teachers and guides of the race, that the turn of the wheel of evolution may now at last be upward. Those who are pressing it upward are the disciples, who are being made by the score in every community instead of one or two arising in it.

And what is it to be a disciple? It is to grow as the flower grows; and to do that, it is necessary to become as the flower. A seedling must spring up within the human heart capable of producing that lotus flower which blooms upon the waters of the sacred tank—the *chakra* which is the correspondence to the brain, in the ethereal form. When the physical brain is stilled and silenced for ever the flower of the soul blooms on upon the still water, undisturbed by that which men call death.

Infinite patience and great endurance are necessary for this inner production, this growth and flowering of the soul. Every work of art, every natural growth requires these two qualities throughout their production. How much more so a work above art, a growth beyond nature! The path of Occultism is shorter than the long pilgrimage of learning from life only; but it seems very long to those who are entering upon it, because each step has to be right and true. There is no passing on with faltering or uncertain footsteps; any wavering leads to the darkness. The great disciples or learners are those who are anxious not merely to find freedom for themselves, but to help on evolution, and they do not hesitate to pay the inevitable price of intensified discipline. For discipline is an essential part of discipleship, from the first step to the last; not one step can be taken without the discipline which arises from it and belongs to it.

To become a disciple means that a man must will to become one. The choice of direction arises from free will, not from *karma*. No one is called to discipleship. The ego of itself approaches it. By the same law no teacher or master seeks his disciple; he only comes when he is called, and is required. To be a disciple does not imply learning from a teacher or master. The word means only the desire and power of learning, and a disciple may be self-taught, or may learn the lessons of life. The ordinary man does not wish to learn the lessons of life; he kicks against the pricks, grasps at personal possessions, and demands comfort and pleasure. The difference between his state of mind and that of the disciple is caused by the desire to learn. The disciple, having this object before him, does not resent the suffering resulting from the lessons which form the discipline of life. He accepts the lessons, and the suffering, as a necessary part of his training, and sees no injustice or cruelty in the orderings of *karma*. Rather than resent the fate that falls upon him or seek to escape it, he sheds the blood of the heart. The disciple longs for the consciousness of this condition, and willingly enters upon the torture which eventually enables him to stand in the presence of the Masters. The undisciplined nature desires to avoid all that is painful and to seize upon pleasure with both hands. Thus all training, all development, is made impossible. No seedling which shall bring forth a sacred flower is sown in a grasping and rebellious heart. But, be it remembered, the whole object of human life is the training of incarnated souls; and therefore the rebel in life is punished by the action of the laws of life, just as the deserter is punished by military law. It is very much easier to escape from military law—even if by suicide—than from the laws of life; these indeed are inexorable.   He that will not learn will suffer exceedingly, just as the child suffers exceedingly who persists in testing the burning power of fire.

The disciple not only will learn, but wills to learn ; and, knowing that nothing can be learned without pain, wills to suffer, indeed asks for training and discipline even if it involves suffering.   Witness Christina Rossetti's cry in " From House to Home " :

> " Although to-day He prunes my twigs with pain
>   Yet doth His blood nourish and warm my root,
>
>   To-morrow I shall put forth buds again,
>   And clothe myself in fruit."

This is the true attitude of the disciple, one who seeks for "home."

It is remarkable that nature and the nature spirits know nothing of discipline apart from man.   Their evolution belongs to a different order.   But they are man's true friends and willing servants, and in his service they submit to discipline.   Only for man's use do fruit trees need to be pruned with pain; only in man's service do the animals need to endure training and punishment.

The perfection of the disciple is a different matter from the perfection of a man—if such a thing could be. But it cannot be, for man perfected is no longer man, and passes onward. But the steps of the disciple must needs be perfect and fully completed, as must the works of artists. And there is a technique in the conduct of the disciple, colouring in a certain manner all his life, as there is a technique which marks the artist. The school to which he belongs is known to those who are able to look intelligently upon him ; but it is no earthly school. The perfection of an artist's work, or the perfection of a disciple's steps, does not mean that this mastery or successful accomplishment makes *the man* perfect. As man, all he can do is to choose his direction and follow it unwaveringly. The growth of the disciple arises within the man, and it is that which is the flower of his nature ; and it is that which grows as the flower grows.

As I wrote these words a rose in a vase fell and all the petals scattered themselves over the page on which the ink was wet. It was so unexpected that it seemed as if the rose must have been touched. Was it to remind me that now is the place to explain what has hitherto received no attention in written words—that the flower opens itself

2

eagerly to the air and gazes upon the sun—
and falls.

Disciplehood is impermanent like man-
hood.

The flower of the sacred lotus opens upon
the water of the "sacred tank" (that *chakra*
which is the correspondence of the brain),
and according to its power and strength it
remains for a length of time, the glory of
the disciple, and the wonder of all who gaze
upon it. In course of time the petals fall and
the head droops. Ah! but the fragrance of
those fallen petals! It makes the world the
sweeter, and it ascends to the higher worlds
heralding the coming of a great soul.

The general idea taken from the words
"grow as the flower grows" is, that an easy
mode of development is suggested, all things
natural being usually regarded as easy. We
are so ignorant in respect to Nature that we
imagine no effort or pain belongs to her
experiences. We simply do not know anything about it; all we know, or consider, is
to have the flowers we want produced in the
garden we possess. But the highly advanced
Yogin who can enter into the being and consciousness of that which he gazes upon knows
whether the flower is aware of effort when it

opens its petals, and whether it suffers when they fall.

To grow as the flower grows it is necessary to become as a flower, and everything that flowers springs out of the earth, from its seedling source. What of that great effort of raising itself from the place whence it draws its original strength? Do not forget the vital importance of that dark soil. It is easy to despise the physical plane and the material life, as is the way with some students; it is not so easy to grow out of them. For growth is not a matter of a single effort, or a violent one; it is accomplished by ceaseless patient endeavour in one direction—upward. And any little shaking or disturbance of the roots affects the well-being of the whole plant or tree. The hold upon that from which the flower rises must be deep, strong, unshaken. When a plant is transplanted, however skilfully, a little illness is caused, from which it has to recover before it can proceed with its great effort. The root of the disciple is planted in human love, friendship, and affection; he cannot loose his hold on these while raising himself to gaze on the Supreme, or his head would droop, and his strength would fail. To maintain the perfect equipoise means perfect discipline. Often the twigs are pruned with pain, sometimes the roots are pruned by a skilful gardener. There is, of necessity, suffering as well as pleasure.

And what of the undisciplined? For them the suffering is severe, because they kick against its pricks. For them the cup of bitterness is filled to the brim and they have to drink it to the dregs, because they do not reach towards the cup of the Holy Grail. Not for them the dish of the sacrament, or the vessel in which the blood of Christ crucified is poured out. The Christos of man, crucified on the pairs of opposites, sheds that which is the blood of the Son of God, for the soul of man to drink—ay, and to drink to the dregs. But the soul of man must desire to know the meaning of this sacred sacrament before it can redeem him and make all life glorious. The sacrament was given to the disciples, the learners, then but few.

CHAPTER II

"ATTEND YOU TO THEM"

ATTENTION has within it the idea of stretching or reaching out, and of this act being continuous. There are many modes of listening, of giving heed, of watching, that do not contain this idea, which is an essential part of the word attention.

Children are told to attend at school, and to attend to their lessons. They evade school when possible and their lessons are forgotten so soon as they leave school. (I write as an Englishwoman of the system of training children in my country.)

A nurse watching her patient may sleep for a few moments when the invalid is at rest. The mother or nurse watching an infant may do needlework or read a book when the child is asleep or playing safely. The mechanic watching a machine can talk to his mates when it is busy at work.

The soldier on duty, when all is quiet, can

for a moment relax the strain and think of his friends at home.

Not so the disciple. He is told *to attend*, which means continuous stretching out, unrelaxing effort.

The nurse who sleeps for a little while simply rests.

The disciple is even more active in dream-consciousness than in the physical consciousness, and though sleep is a rest to the physical brain it does not for an instant release the disciple from his continuous stretching out of attention. Always, sleeping or waking, he listens for the voice that is soundless; he gazes on that which is invisible; he directs himself towards that which is beyond reach. And unless he does so he is not a disciple. For the disciple is told to *attend* to the rules of life and development. He is not told to attend to them at certain hours, or in certain places, but always. And these rules cover the whole of life, control every action and every thought.

"ATTEND YOU TO THEM"

I cannot point out in this chapter what this injunction means; it requires the whole of the interpretation to do so. I desire now only to show what these simple words convey —the stretching out and reaching towards, unceasingly, the order of development directed in these mystic rules. The whole of life, in all the consciousnesses, is covered by them. There is not a single thing, however slight or small, which can be done without attention to them. They touch every point of experience, every development of life, and they flood the whole with a new meaning, and a new passion. The ecstasy of the disciple, which transforms all that is sordid and severe into that which is superb and delightful, arises from *attention* to these rules. The habit has to be acquired of undertaking nothing however small or large, or performing no act, whether simple or great, without reference to these rules. It will soon be found that all undertakings and all acts come definitely under one or another of them, and the way of action is dictated inexorably and unmistakably. Attention to this dictation gives to the disciple new power and new insight. Confirmed attention takes the disciple into the inner meanings of life and the profound abysses of experience.

CHAPTER III

THE MASTERS

THE preliminary stanzas have the singular characteristic that the Masters are not mentioned in the two first, while they dominate the two last. Attention to this reveals that the two first stanzas govern the first part of the rules, in which the Masters are not concerned. This preparation has to be accomplished by the disciple unaided, and is indeed purely a matter of choosing directions. A great change comes at the end of this first part, when the disciple is told *to ask*. And with this great change comes the entrance into that greater consciousness which is described in the second part. First comes the Warrior, the Higher Self; and then the Holy Ones of the earth become accessible. These are the first Masters who appear upon the way, and they can only be approached by the Higher Self. They dwell in the inner states of the physical plane where that which corresponds to the Higher Self of man, in all plants and animals, can be encountered and perceived. It is here that the disciple makes his study of the mystery of the being and action of earth, air, and water. This study cannot be made on the physical plane where the vestment of the spirit of all things can alone be perceived, and that only by the use of a physical organ. It is necessary to withdraw into an interior condition where the warrior, the higher self, can enter into communion with the higher self of that which is being studied. Therefore it may truly be said that the Higher Self is literally the first Master encountered on the way, for it is necessary that this should take command, and that the personality, the incarnated part of the ego, should take his orders and obey them. This means the surrender of all personal desires, even in some cases the elimination of characteristics of the personality which have been brought by *karma* from a past incarnation, for the personality has to stand aside in the battle of life, and let the Warrior be that which fights. That means the total change which can only be expressed as being that from the state of the ordinary man to that of the disciple.

The Higher Self of the man is therefore to be recognised as his first Master, whose orders are to be obeyed implicitly, more implicitly than the orders of a General are obeyed by his soldiers. For this obedience is not merely the result of discipline, but also of absolute surrender. No shadow of doubt can arise as to the wisdom of the orders of the Warrior, for he is thyself, convinced, enlightened, illuminated. There can be no question as to his wisdom or his right to command. The soldier obeys commands, the wisdom of which he may doubt; he may consider that the General whom he obeys is not well fitted for that particular post of command. His obedience is automatic and the result of discipline only. Such a situation cannot arise between the disciple and the Warrior, therefore these words are written, "Obey him, not as though he were a General." The obedience has to be unquestioning and without doubt, and will be so as soon as the Higher Self is recognised. He rules as the absolute Master.

Under his guidance the inner senses can be developed with safety; but not until he rules. The reason of the danger of spiritualism is that it is practised by those who are not disciples, who have not recognised the Warrior, who are untrained and unguided. Only when the inner senses are developed under his control is it time to enter upon the study of the world, visible and invisible, in which we live. This study has to be accomplished before we can be released from rebirth. For everything the disciple passes through and experiences has to be understood by him ; each experience constitutes a step. So in the battle of life and the lessons arising from it — unutterable joys, intense ordeals, fiery sacrifices, and sufferings, which come of contact with other souls that are in the vortex—the ordinary man learns or refuses to learn the lessons. That is all he can attempt. The disciple has to do much more than that ; he has not only to learn the lessons, but to understand them. He may not give up a problem which has come into his own life, and say that it is beyond his understanding. He has to look upon it till he sees the truth in respect to it. This is done under the guidance of his own Higher Self, his first teacher. So soon as the Warrior is implicitly obeyed, without resistance, questioning, or doubt, when He has conquered the desires of the outer senses, then he finds his

way to the Holy Ones of the earth to inquire
of them the secrets they hold for him.   The
Higher Self and the personality have now
become one, and go on the path without
hesitation.   The search for the Masters from
whom truth can be learned then commences;
and the demand for teaching is made.   It is
then at once realised that there are succes-
sive orders of Masters at the service of the
disciples.   The first of these Orders encountered on the path is the small one of
the Holy Ones of the earth.   This is formed
of those who have a great sense of purity
and honour, but who have not gained the
impetus which raises a soul into the higher
planes of the ethereal world between the incarnations.   They serve man close at hand
because they are so very human that they
can serve him best there.   In the midst of a
certain number of men (a number known to
the adepts) one of these is embodied, and
rises up as a teacher of high morality, pure
living, honour, and truth.   They may appear,
and do so appear, in any of the churches, or
they may be leaders in any form of public
life, for their teaching is above, and irre-
spective of, any doctrine or school of thought.
It arises from the consciousness within them-

selves of the need that man shall learn to
live rightly and to think rightly. They
clearly know right from wrong in all human
actions. Their responsibility is very great,
as in their varied positions as priests, pastors,
authors, poets, teachers of the young, leaders
of all kinds, they draw towards them the
crowds of men and women who are beginning to perceive the Warrior, who are
beginning to look for the path. They hold
secrets which they alone can impart ; for
none enters that order of Masters who has
not paid dearly for the right to do so.
Theirs is a very special work, not in any
sense an experience necessary for disciples to
undertake, nor possible for men in general
to enter into. Sin stands ever before their
eyes as the greatest menace to man. *Karma*
brings to them those who are stumbling over
the same steps which they have stumbled
over and have eventually surmounted. They
are usually passionate devotees; always fervid
and eager souls, full of devotion and self-
sacrifice. You are not told to follow them
into the religious creeds or the schools of
thought to which they belong and which they
represent on earth, but to inquire of them the
secrets they hold *for you*. Some impetus

given to the Higher Self, some new light on thought and actions will come of contact with one of these Holy Ones. And your path will certainly cross the path of such an one sooner or later. Possibly a whole incarnation may be passed in grasping and bringing into action the secret he holds for you; and in that case you will probably enter into the church or school which he represents. But being a disciple who has definitely entered on the path you will not be hindered or cramped by doctrine or modes of thought. Between the incarnations these masters themselves are freed from such limitations. They remain close to the earth on which their work lies, close to man whom they serve, but are under the teaching of the higher Masters, and in their schools learn to shake off the shackles of earthly modes of thought. The lower planes of the ethereal world holds many such schools.

There is country of the most exquisite beauty on these planes, and deep woodlands full of peace. Secluded in the heart of such a woodland a temple is often hidden, screened from all but those whose aspirations lead them to it. When a certain number of disciples have found the sheltered path which leads to it the door closes. For here are never crowded assemblies. An unseen guardian (unseen to those who enter because of possessing a more spiritualised form than theirs) shuts the temple completely to the outer consciousness when enough have entered. These being practised students, most often Holy Ones of the earth, either in the state of dream-consciousness or between the incarnations, remain still in the place they chose on entering. And presently the Master who is to teach them is there, standing among them. He comes from a higher state, and enters the temple in another manner than they do. They do not know how he comes; but they know when he is there. Most often he belongs to the Order of the Brotherhood of Love. It is the teaching of that Order which is greatly needed by the Holy Ones of the earth, whose tendency, from their peculiar conditions and mode of training, is towards austerity, and limitation of thought and feeling. In this time of universal and worldwide trial and suffering very, very often it is the Christ Himself, the *Avatar*, the Great Master, who, when two or three are gathered together, is found to be standing there in the

midst of them.   The Order of the Brotherhood of Love is to be regarded as specially
under the guidance of the Christ and in
charge of His flocks, for the reason that
its members have willingly surrendered the
delight of dwelling in the heavens during
the long periods between their incarnations,
in order to maintain their influence on the
thought force of humanity and in the hearts
of men.   They have their homes in the
ethereal heights, but they seldom enter
them, save for occasional rest and refresh-
ment at the fount of spiritual life.   They
preserve without cessation the continuity of
the Love Litany, chanting it by the altar of
the Hall of Learning always.   Men, who in
dream-consciousness hear it, go about the
world in physical consciousness with hearts
full of joy, no matter what sorrow and
suffering surrounds them.   The members of
this Order make a great sacrifice for the
sake of humanity, following the example of
the Christ, who promised to remain with us
to the end of the Eon, and who has never
left us.   They incarnate at long intervals,
for their own training and experience. They
are never teachers upon earth, their knowledge being too spiritual to enter into men's

minds through the action of thought. Spoken words cannot express that which they have to give to others. Their incarnations are usually lives either of great suffering or of strenuous effort, so gloriously encountered by means of the spirit of love they hold within them that the impetus from it carries them to that high place, the enjoyment of which they surrender in order to remain with the Good Shepherd in the interior life, close to His sheep. The members of those Orders of Masters beyond and above this Order do not make any sacrifice in their service to man, because they are beyond the laws of *karma* and rebirth, and many of them have only incarnated once in prehistoric ages when the earth was pure, and will not incarnate again until she is purified. They seldom come into contact with the spirits of men who are incarnated, their tasks consisting in strange and marvellous manipulations of the forces of life, of the guiding of national *karma*, of the evolution of races, and development of racial instincts. They instruct the Masters below them, and some advanced disciple, or disciples who have special work given them to do on earth, are enabled to see them

when at work and to have their work explained. In such a manner is it (in connection with work given me to do) that since
this period of strife and suffering has set in
I have been allowed on several occasions to
see Masters of the higher Orders guiding
and guarding the threads of the *karma* of
the world, and watching the great wheel of
evolution.   Man   is   watched   and   helped
always ; never is he left to struggle alone.

There are many more such orders than I
know of, rising up and up, to the verge of
pure spirit. I cannot give the name of any
Order above that of the Brotherhood of
Love, nor do I know the functions of any
higher Order. I only know of members of
high Orders whom I have been enabled to
see at work or who have given to me some
special help when I was out of the body
seeking guidance. I can only say that it is
certain that man is never deserted, never
lost. He has only to look up, to reach upward, to *give attention* to that which is
higher than himself, and he will find *One*
ready to help him, *One* who descends in
order to do so, and who draws him upward
by the power of attraction.

The Masters remain always mysterious,

for they are always beyond and above the disciple. It is possible, indeed probable, that the disciple will not clearly perceive a master who has helped him. Sometimes, if the effort being made is very severe, more than one master helps that aspirant, who perhaps never perceives them clearly, but is only conscious of their power to help.

There is a very high Egyptian Master of whom I know, and whose house I know, for I was taken there at the time when the world-war was at its little beginning, and I was allowed to see the Seeresses reading the prophecies in the mystic water which told how great and protracted a war was upon us. I possess an Egyptian scarab which I felt sure contained a charm or some special power, and I earnestly desired to discover what this might be. I asked to be instructed in this; and I was taken to the house of the Egyptian master which I had visited before — a visit described in the *Crucible*. The scarab, I knew, came from the tomb of a certain Egyptian king; its authenticity was accepted by Egyptian experts. I was told that only the Ka of that king could tell me the charm that lay in the ring, and that I must seek him in the tomb. I was taken to the house of the Egyptian master (on the ethereal plane) and, passing through the interior of it (much of the detail I perceived and clearly remember), came, at the end of a long corridor, to the open door of a perfectly dark room. I was told to enter, and after being in it a few moments I became able to see, and saw that three masters sat there in silence. In their midst was a dais over which hung a crystal that sometimes appeared to be a living flame. I was made to understand that the three masters had been talking to very high spiritual beings who came in the flame, and appeared upon the dais.

I was told to stand on the dais, and was given a crystal to hold in my hand. Through it, by the help of the masters present, I passed into another and deeper consciousness. In that deeper consciousness I found myself in the tomb of the Egyptian king from which the ring had been taken ; my face was close against the carved stone of the side of his coffin. It was the ethereal counterpart of that tomb, for as his Ka suddenly arose and stood beside me I saw the counterpart of the scarab. Let none imagine the ethereal to be cloudy, vague, or without solidity. The sun in that world shines more brightly than the physical sun, all nature colouring is more vivid and beautiful than that of which it is the counterpart, and the sense of firmness and solidity is very great. The stone against which I leaned was stone indeed. The tall terrible figure that stood beside me filled me—not with fear — but with overpowering awe. Awful though it was, this presence gave me the deepest sense I have ever had of certainty and of security. A voice came—slow and deep—and I was told that the power of the scarab was that of work and accomplishment. A few more words, personally to myself, were uttered, and then I slipped back from one inner consciousness to another less deep, till I returned to my physical body, crouched in a chair beside a dying wood fire. How unreal this world looks after an effort towards the great realities was brought home to me. I have only once since made that same effort, in February 1916, when I reached the tomb again, to hear only one sentence uttered by the awe-inspiring presence—the ominous words, "*England is being sold like a bean in the market.*"

I only dimly perceived the three Masters whose presence enabled me to enter into this deep state of consciousness. I know not their names nor the Order to which they belong. I give this illustration only to show how varied is the nature of the help they give to disciples, and how hard is the task sometimes, so that one Master alone cannot accomplish it.

I know that there is one very high Order whose sole work is leading men to gaze upon the Supreme, and to regard that as their goal. They influence men through other masters nearer to humanity, and draw them to the one great end as by a magnet.

CHAPTER IV

"SIGHT"

"Before the eyes can see they must be incapable
of tears."

THIS very first stanza has been a source
of much perplexity to students, and
has been frequently misinterpreted. By the
misinterpretation of this preliminary statement the whole text becomes misleading and
obscure.

It is necessary to remember that all words
used in it are used in their occult sense, not
in their ordinary sense. It is also necessary
to remember that it is the disciple who is
being addressed in the rules, not the ordinary man. These two facts release the
student from the danger of supposing that
human feeling and human love are to be
eliminated from the nature of man. The
disciple is that mystic nature which arises
within the man, and comes to its flowering in

39

his interior life, but its root and power upon
earth are deeply planted in human feeling,
and in human love.

The prehistoric yoga, which bears the
name of the Persian sage "Patanjali" because he first put it into written words, con-
tains the needed explanation of this first
stanza. I must quote a little from *The Transparent Jewel*, or it would seem to students of
that book that this is mere repetition.

The aphorisms which throw light on this
first stanza of *Light on the Path* are XX.
and XXI. of Book II. :

> "XX. The seer is vision simply, though
> pure, looking directly on ideas.
> "XXI. The being of the sight is for him."

When "the eyes can see" indicates that
state of the disciple, now a highly advanced
yogin, when he has become "The seer, or
vision simply." In that state he obtains full
and complete knowledge of the phenomenal
universe, which is "the sight," that which he
looks on. That the "being of the sight is
for him" means in more explanatory language that the whole phenomenal universe
has been called into existence solely for the
experience and development of the soul of

man. In the next aphorism it is explained that it no longer exists for the freed soul, for "him whose purpose has been fulfilled," but it still exists for others.

"Sight" (page 89, *The Transparent Jewel*) "is all which is seen by the spirit in the objective world, including the substance and organs and senses of the very body used by the spirit, its higher mentality, and the egoism which causes its individuality. The spirit is stripped of all its sheaths and vestures in its capacity as the seer; these sheaths and vestures are themselves a part of that which it looks upon—*the sight*."

The expression is used in the sense in which we speak of some beautiful view or great pageant, "a wonderful sight"—"a sight to see"—the occult sense within it being that "the sight" is *all* phenomenal objects, in their hidden and interior conditions. The Yogin can, in the language of the Persian teacher, "throw the light of immediate cognition" on any object of sense, whether "minute, concealed, or distant"—whether on the earth, or in the space between the earth and the sun, or in the starry regions, or within the physical body of the Yogin himself.

This is the "seeing" of the first aphorism of *Light on the Path*, and before the disciple reaches to that great power of obtaining knowledge, all grief, all sorrow and sighing have passed away from him because he knows the truth; and the tears have been wiped from his eyes for ever. In rebirth again, bearing the cross of human experience once more, he will retain the mystic knowledge of the saint, "Juliana of Norwich," that "all shall be well—all shall be well—and all manner of thing shall be well." This state is followed by that in which the "sight" no longer exists for the freed soul. The following paragraph from *The Transparent Jewel* (page 89) explains the conditions of this new state very briefly: "The five *Tattvas* form the fivefold field of evolution. In the Buddhist books four elements are spoken of: air, fire, water, and earth. In the Hindu philosophy there are five, which correspond to sound, touch, sight, taste, and smell. The visible universe is apprehended by these senses, which become aware of the elements and the phenomena arising from their activity. The use of this fivefold field is the development or absolution of the spirit, the seer. So soon as the spirit perceives the

All-Soul, he has no further need for the manifested life."

Be it remembered that though the Yogin or highly advanced disciple may have no further need of the fivefold field of manifested life for himself, he will work for those who need it, either from a near or a far distance, according to his condition, because the object of all who know the truth is the liberation of the whole human race. For it is a united body which must pass through the gate of freedom all together.

Patanjali explains in the third book of his Yoga Aphorisms how sight is developed by the seer. It must be clearly understood that *before* this development is possible that state has to be attained in which sorrow and sighing are past, and all tears wiped away for ever. Life must be regarded from an interior consciousness, where the Brotherhood of Love fills the heart with unutterable joy, and from which the state of grief and pain is seen as one of the pairs of opposites. Man is perceived as perfectly free to pass out of this condition of crucifixion, if he will call upon the Warrior and by his aid enter upon the path.

Definite teaching from a Master of the

Order of the Brotherhood of Love, who will enable the disciple to enter the great peace, is necessary in order to attain this state. This attained, it is possible, under the guidance of a Master of another Order, to enter upon the development of sight. The Sanskrit word for the condition required for seeing is *Samayama*, which means the conquest of the lower mind and senses. This condition has to be so perfected as to have become natural. "A discerning principle" or "sight" is by this means developed. The "Three *Yogangas*" are necessary for its use—"attention, contemplation, and meditation." When "attention" is fixed upon the object to be seen, the trance state called in Sanskrit *Samadhi* arises, and the Yogin enters into the very nature of objects, and becomes able to understand them in their very essence. By giving "attention" to *Jyotis* (the light in the head) he enters into the state in which he can see divine personages, adepts, or spirits.

From this power of discerning the subtle and the hidden, an immense and unimaginable tide of pleasure flows in upon the disciple ; and therefore, although it is essential that it should be fully experienced, when made perfect it becomes "an obstacle in the way," and must be left behind with all other forms of pleasure.   So absorbing is the interest and delight of the study of both sight and hearing, that the Yogin will pass years in a trance condition gazing on the wonders of the phenomenal world, and needs arousing by the call of these Masters who urge him to use his power for gazing on the Supreme.

CHAPTER V

"HEARING"

"Before the ear can hear it must have lost its
sensitiveness."

IT is clear from the context that the sensitiveness here spoken of is that which is
aware of pain.

We are told in the mystic Book of Revela-
tion that when all tears are wiped away, also
there shall never be any more pain. Those
who dwell with their God in the new earth
have attained that state where there is neither
sorrow nor crying, for nothing can any longer
cause pain. The ear has lost its sensitiveness, and the source of suffering being
eliminated, the hearing opens itself to receive
the sounds of the song of life. Death being
swallowed up in victory, it is evident that
physical pain is not referred to, but that pain
which comes even to souls of love from
hearing the cry of the suffering world. They

46

may themselves perceive that pain is only one arm of the cross, but they know that the world does not understand the mystery of the Crucifixion and a " passion of compassion " falls on them and threatens to overwhelm all else.

"A divine organ of hearing is developed in the Yogin by his performing Samayama with regard to the connection between the organ of hearing and the ether " (Patanjali Yoga Aphorism XLI. Book III.).

This is the whole matter, stated very simply. Included in that simple statement are colossal facts, and most advanced occult conditions are referred to. These are previously explained in the Yoga Aphorisms. To begin with, the Yogin is in himself a colossal fact—he can exist, he does exist, he is a fact, yet he is so far removed from the ordinary man as to seem like a phantasy and a legendary being. Not so—he moves in realities, sterner and more intense realities than those encountered by the ordinary man. The Yogin is that disciple who has so completely conquered the lower mind and senses that the state of conquest has become a normal and natural condition. He is able to

use the three *Yogangas* in such a manner
that he can listen to the sounds of the
ethereal world, and lose all sensitiveness to
those sounds which cause suffering to the
one who hears, because they express the pain
and grief of mankind. He can listen to the
song of life, that mysterious and unceasing
melody of which the music of the spheres is
a part. He can learn from the lesson of
harmony, having so far progressed in his
development that he can recognise harmony
as being triumphant over all discord. Every
natural sound is part of the divine harmony,
but he has long since gone past that place of
experience, and now hears the divine harmony
of the vibrations of the universe. This
divine harmony belongs to the second of the
three forms of cosmic manifestation : that of
rhythmical expression of purity and truth.
All that is lovely in human nature, all the
illumination and spirituality of man is repre-
sented in its perfect rhythm and melody.
Sound is caused in the highest of the five
fields of evolution which are spoken of by
the Sanskrit writers—*Akasha*, the most spiritual form of the primordial substance. This
condition is as nearly a state of pure spirit
as anything within the phenomenal universe

can be. It is beyond and above the ethereal world or Buddhic state. The sight and hearing of the disciple are powers drawn from that spiritual state and exercised in it.

CHAPTER VI

"SPEECH"

THE Sanskrit teachers have given us the conception of the phenomenal universe (or fivefold field of evolution) as the result of three forms of cosmic manifestation—darkness, light, and action. We are told in the Bhagavad Gîtâ (xiv. 7) that the manifestation of actions or energy is the passion nature, and is the source of attachment to and thirst for life.

From the story told in Genesis of the creations of the universe we learn how these three manifestations were called into existence by speech.

In the language of occultism speech is creation, or that manifestation of the ego which takes an outward form.

It is accepted by all schools of occultists that there is a quality of resistance in the phenomenal world which retards the play of life, consciousness, or spirit. From it comes inertia, indifference, ignorance, insensibility, stagnatism, and darkness ; all or any of these words can be used as a translation of the Sanskrit word for it (*tamas*). "It is the absence of all knowledge, feeling, motion, transparency. It is one of the forms of the great illusion—it is not eternal. It "drops off when liberation is attained." From it comes all that is known among men as evil, or sin. This, being impermanent, is not a part of the mystic creation of the world from which arises all the permanent and perfected qualities and states of the redeemed and liberated spirit of man. The spirit of the Creator moved upon the formless darkness and said, "Let there be light." By that speech He not only brought into existence all that is beautiful and good in the phenomenal universe, but He created the first great pair of opposites, and inaugurated the condition of crucifixion in which the spirit of man was to be taught and developed. Some Indian schools declare that this Creating Spirit so far sacrificed Himself for the sake of the human race that He Himself submitted to the state of Duality and became Two instead of One, thus Himself entering into the Crucifixion.

By speech He called Light into being ; and
then by speech He called forth all the
phenomena of activity and energy which have
become known to us as the fivefold field of
evolution ; the highest state of light or the
spiritual world known to the purified spirits
of men ; the field, or world, or plane below
it, known to some schools as the Buddhic
plane ; the Sanskrit name for it means
" purification." It is there that purified
souls, still subject to rebirth, find their home
between the incarnations. From thence
come the causes of the air and the wind, and
there dwells their personified principle, the
great being who brings vitality into the
lower worlds. There is the " substrate of the
sensation of touch." The next " field " is
that of the ethereal world which is more or
less known by practical experience to disciples
and occultists. Below that is the astral
world, in which " actions " and desires are
powerful ; and below that the physical world
of matter, the Sanskrit word for which means
simply the earth. The Creator made man in
His own image, " And God said, Let us
make man in our own Image, after our likeness "—this speech certainly containing the
idea that He was dual and had consented to

enter into crucifixion for the sake of that race of beings for whom He was creating a place of experience and evolution. It also implies and declares that man possesses this power. Man also is a creator and has the great gift of speech.

The Creator called into being within the fivefold field the many sentient creatures who have dwelt in it from then till now, as the friends of man, round whom they were gathered. Their spirits had dwelt elsewhere, as had man's; for all spirit is eternal. They were called by uttered words to come into forms in the place made for man, and when he was called into being he was given dominion over those on the earth. But he was not told that he might kill them or devour them. To him and them alike green herbs were given for food. It is quite clear from the story given in Genesis that the animal creation and its evolution, while it companions man's, is not in any sense the same as his. No animal is created in the likeness of the creator. All the beings of the animal kingdom follow their own laws and take their own path, while remaining with man in his fivefold field. They do not enter into his morality or his religion or his evolution; they only love him and serve him.

The accomplished and "confirmed" state of disciplehood admits the inner man to all the mystic glories of the universe. To the one who has just entered on the way that state is the goal; and this is the reason why in the Patanjali Yoga aphorism the end is given before the beginning. The moment the disciple has entered the path the point of *direction* becomes of vital and unceasing importance. Tolstoi set it down as the one thing that matters; so indeed it is, for a disciple who is sure of his direction cannot take a false step. Therefore is it that he listens always for that which is soundless, and gazes always on that which is invisible, and recognises the Supreme as that to which the path he has chosen must eventually lead him. He knows also that illumination may at any moment be instantaneous, so that time does not trouble him nor the need of patience weary him. For the need of patience may cease suddenly, and concerning time he knows that it is not a reality. Beyond the fivefold field it does not exist at all; and in the ethereal world to which he soon obtains entrance he finds the Masters who have the three times as one—past, present, and future being visible to them as a whole.

As soon as the disciple takes his first step upon the path, all actions great and small change in character. With the ordinary man action is caused by desire, and arises in the field just above the physical field of life— that which is called astral. Here passion, hatred, theft (in the occult sense), ambition, selfishness spring like strong weeds and cover the ground as the yellow charlock covers the fields of England and France in war-time, when men must shed blood instead of weeding and tilling the soil of their native countries. The ordinary man has to learn, as a gardener learns, the difference between the valuable plant and the weed which is useless and which chokes all else ; in fact, the difference between right and wrong. And it is in this that the Holy Ones of the earth are able to help him, for the righteousness of the earth is theirs.

The disciple follows the law of the flower ; from the moment he decides to rise up from earth and open to the spiritual sun he steadily grows upward. And from that moment his every action becomes speech, and is recognised by those who are watching from the ethereal and spiritual worlds, as manifesting there. He, in fact, acts in such a manner that he calls into being forms in these states, which are known as emanations from him. A wonderful and beautiful phenomenon is that every disciple who arrives, or has arrived, in those clearer and purer worlds, enlarges them and increases their beauty; therefore are these neophytes very welcome, and they are ceaselessly watched for. Just as the gardener looks for the opening bud, so the Master looks for the opening soul.

And disciplehood, though it is an interior growth within the physical man which is formed by *karma*, governs that man entirely. So that from the moment of waking into the world from dream-consciousness or deep-sleep-consciousness, at the dawn of every day, all through that day every action whether great or small is done in the spirit of consecration and according to the law of love.

When the actions are of such a nature that they become manifested in the ethereal and spiritual worlds, then the Masters perceive them. Then it is that the voice of the disciple can speak in the presence of the Masters; he can then call forms into being which give joy and satisfaction to those

great Ones.   For every action creates a
form.

These forms are small and slight; for the
disciple is only just beginning to hear and
see in the world in which he desires to make
his voice heard.   But with the first faint
dawn of understanding of what hearing and
sight are, all possibilities arise.   The flowering has begun.

The word Masters is used in the plural
because it is not that one, or any appointed
Master, hears the speech of the disciple.   It
is that according to the impetus given to the
spirit of the disciple by his actions on the
lower fields of evolution, so he reaches to one
or another of the higher fields.   His speech
may reach to the presence of a Master in the
ethereal world, or to a Master in the spiritual
world according to the force and selflessness
of his action.   All Masters are ready to hear
him, and welcome the sound of his voice.

CHAPTER VII

STABILITY

THE disciple is taught to stand, by his first Master, the Warrior within him. Before he attempts to go beyond the teaching of his own higher self, he has to learn to stand upright and firm as a rock amid "the turmoil" and in "the battle," which is the result of the vortex of human life on the physical plane. No suffering, no grief, no trouble affects the purpose or direction of a truly strong man or woman in whom the higher self rules. These stand out among weaklings, or people of uncertain purpose; nothing can turn them aside from that which is right and true. We know and recognise these self-contained and self-controlled ones in all walks and orders of ordinary human life. They have taken that first step which makes them as rocks amid waves. No small things can move them; only great issues claim their attention. It is not the gentle or timid souls who can go upon the path ; it is the resolute and firm who have learned to stand against the shocks and buffetings of life. Therefore do not look to find the disciple in places of ease ; his powers of endurance have to be tested in the simplest of the fivefold fields before he essays to enter upon those above it.

The race of mankind has its foothold on the earth in physical life. And the feet with which he stands or moves on earth must be washed in the blood of the heart before he can stand in the presence of the Masters. The higher self is that which stands, keeping its hold upon physical life by dominating its bodily form. And when it has acquired power and strength by standing amid the turmoil of this lowest field of action, it desires to make the great essay, and finds it can only do so by destroying those weeds which grow richly in the two lower fields of its nature. It is not grief or sorrow or suffering which makes the heart of the Warrior bleed ; he has taught himself to endure these unshaken. It is the drawing out of the heart the source of evil and expunging it. This is like drawing the very life-blood, and often it may seem too great a strain upon the whole nature to be endured. Ambition is the most subtle and most violent temptation of those who have acquired strength. Therefore is it placed as the first weed to be drawn forth from the heart, causing it to bleed.

PART II

THE TRANSMUTATION OF DESIRE

CHAPTER I

THE TRANSMUTATION OF DESIRE

AMBITION, desire of comfort, and desire of life—these three deep fundamental desires of man, which are essential to the human race, have a twofold form of energy. They are therefore capable of being submitted to ordeal, of being burnt in the crucible of human life, and in that crucible transmuted from their human form of energy to its divine counterpart. That is the meaning of the first four rules of the text.

Ambition is so deeply rooted in the nature of all aspirants that it may be regarded as the first cause of human life. It is the mystic inner form of ambition which leads the spirit into the physical world and causes desire of life. Desire of life is that which brings him into physical being. What is called life in this text is the life wave of the third Logos which outpours into the fivefold field. The Logoi are "words" or creative forces, and the spirits whom we learn to know as egos, or spirits of men, must be fired by a mysterious form of ambition in order to become a part of the outpouring and to enter consciously into the Ray which penetrates and shields them throughout the experiences of birth and rebirth. The "Word of life" is "manifested" (John) in every human being.

Ambition is therefore the first of the great weeds which flourish in human nature and has to be uprooted though it make the heart to bleed—and indeed the roots must be so entirely drawn out that the heart must bleed. But this may not be done until disciplehood is attained, until the Warrior has control and has inquired of the Holy Ones of the earth as to right and wrong. Until then ambition is the great stimulus to action, and raises men out of darkness or inertia. By its help and through its growth they come to a state of activity, which is essential as a preliminary to disciplehood.

Without ambition the turmoil, the battle, which forms the testing in the crucible of man's nature, would not exist. Without ambition there would be no conquest, no civilisation, no statesmen, no politicians, no great soldiers, or great lawyers, or great business men. It enters even into artistic life, and the endeavour to reach the highest point possible leads men into the accomplishing of great feats of workmanship and power. It raises men from the savage state; it fires nations with that passion for power which helps to turn the wheel of evolution. It causes men to conquer their own physical bodies and their weaknesses; it teaches them how to silence the animal nature. For ambition requires the sacrifice of everything but its own object. It has brought the spirit of man into the world of matter, and when transmuted into its higher form it will give him the impetus to retire from the world of matter. He will then become altogether indifferent to place, or power, or recognition; the prizes of physical life are nothing to him, and he is content to be poor and obscure and to walk in the byways of human life. But he is ambitious to obtain his footing in that which is beyond human life, to be recognised by the unseen guides of the race, to appear before the Masters. This impetus is natural and valuable; but if he does not recognise that it is a form of ambition and kill it out in its transmuted form, it will grow stronger and

5

more noxious than before, and stifle his whole being at the last.

The desire of comfort is as deeply rooted in the nature as is ambition. There is desire of expansion, of greater experience, which becomes ambition in the as yet unborn soul; and there is the wish that this expansion and experience should be pleasant, which becomes desire of comfort. Human life is full of pleasant places and of comfort, greatly desired by some who are outside it. It is well known that the elementals desire above all things to enter human life. They can only do so by driving an unstable human soul from its body, and taking its place. Some of them live in madhouses and enjoy it; others become famous "mediums," in the spiritualistic sense. For the elementals can read the thoughts in human minds, as a human being can read a printed page. And they have the three times—past, present, and future—so that they can relate or re-enact events of the past, or foretell those in the future without any effort. They are non-human and without conscience, or scruples as to right or wrong, so that they can draw the utmost out of that comfort which they have so eagerly desired and obtained by theft.

Some who suffer physically think there is little comfort in human life, but those without the pale of the lower of the fivefold fields think otherwise, and would sooner enter any human body than be without one.

Desire of comfort is a great temptation between the incarnations when nearing rebirth. The ordinary man does not attempt to combat it. The wish to enter a healthy, beautiful, perfect body, well placed in the world, appears to him high and natural, and is so for him. But the disciple may have no such wish. He must kill out any such desire. He knows that crucifixion is the law of the evolution into which he has entered, and he embraces pain as gladly as pleasure. To him suffering is sacred, a part of the fiery ordeal which is to result in his purification. Therefore when he approaches rebirth he does not permit himself to desire that he shall have rank, or wealth, or health. He wishes only to work out his *karma* and to do such actions in his lifetime as may become speech in the presence of the Masters.

To kill out desire of life is to surrender the wish for rebirth between the incarnations, and to eliminate the idea which is imprinted

in the mind of the ordinary man during incarnation that his life is his own to be
beloved and guarded and carefully cherished.
It is not his own; it is the result of the
outpouring of the divine vital breath into
matter, and, were that withdrawn, man would
fall prone instantly and no longer exist as
man. It is useless to desire it, in the sense
of guarding the life of a particular incarnation,
because it is withdrawn from an individual
at the bidding of *karma* which dictates to
the gods as well as to men. The common
expression that man cannot die till his hour
has struck expresses the truth as well as any
other words could do. A mystic note is
sounded in the interior spaces where man's
destiny is followed and observed by those
Masters whose task this is, and the out-
breathing on a certain form is withdrawn.
The man's *karma* strikes this note; the
great life-giving force obeys it. And the
man is what is called dead. The great war
has taught to the soldiers themselves and to
the world at large that life and death are not
governed by obvious causes and are not in
the power of other men. The "charmed
life" is well known in the battlefield and
in the munition factories. Death riots there,

but the law remains unbroken that one shall be taken, and another left. Only those whose hour has struck can be destroyed physically by massacre or fire or bombardment. We have seen great soldiers, who had work yet to do, escape death again and again, and recover from wounds which other men die of. One who was seriously wounded had two sets of stretcher-bearers killed as they carried him, and lay under fire. He was brought in, and recovered. Two friends are side by side in an advance—one disappears, so that it can only be supposed he is blown to atoms, the other struck by shrapnel in the throat, and the windpipe avoided by a quarter of an inch—this last one is nursed back quickly into health. Such instances are innumerable; all soldiers know of them. And this law of life and death is gradually being made plain to the fighting forces by sheer experience. It destroys fear. The hardened soldier seems callous to risks. He knows within his inner self, even if he cannot express it, that there are none.

In the Patanjali Yoga the five great vows are given which are the basis of the commandments of the religions of the world.

In the Yoga these vows are stated to be absolutely essential to the disciple "without respect to rank, place, time, or compact." They are the "universal great duty."

The first of these, the most important of all, is *non-killing*, the only English translation which in any way properly represents the Sanskrit word [*non-"himsâ"*]. We find this rule in the Mosaic law as "Thou shalt not kill."

But this is only its first and most elementary meaning. Dividi, a Hindoo commentator of the Patanjali aphorisms, says:

"It is difficult to give the whole import of the word *himsâ* in one word, and I have translated it by 'killing,' for want of a better term. It means the wishing evil to any being by word, act, or thought. It obviously implies abstinence from animal food, inasmuch as it is never procurable without direct or indirect *himsâ* of some kind.

"It is to secure the condition of being ever with nature and never against, or in other words, being in love with nature, that all other restrictions are prescribed.

"Non-killing or perfect and universal compassion" (*The Transparent Jewel*, p. 96) "is the one and only thing strongly prescribed and enjoined—it means nothing less than perfect love, and the attainment of this would naturally result in the keeping of the other commandments or vows, for all mean some kind of wrong action against, or in respect to, others ; and such actions are impossible to one who has attained to perfect and universal compassion."

In the great war now raging (1917), in the wars that have been fought in the past, disciples who are eager to grow upward find themselves compelled by national and personal *karma* to go into the battle with the object of killing.

Do they break their vows by so doing ?

The disciple within the man is freed from *karma*, but not so the man himself ; and he is also a part of that wonderful unit known as a nation. It is a condition of evolution not yet within sight as even conceivable when nations no longer exist. Only those races who aim at the conquest and subjugation of all other races can dream of such a state. Their dream remains a dream because men instinctively knew freedom to be right and true, a state to do battle for.

This being so, the disciple who is a soldier in time of war must know in his interior nature that he is acting rightly. It would be a selfish word uttered in lower regions, not in the presence of the Masters, if he should reject the demand made upon him by his nation for the sake of his own occult advancement; then, even though that advancement be on the path, ambition would be his betrayer, and the cause of failure over a most crucial and difficult step. Do not lose sight of the fact that non-killing is the simplest and most external form of this vow. Love and compassion are the higher forms, and these emanate from him on all sides, affecting not only his actions but his thoughts of all other beings. The disciple who would not give his personality for his nation and as the price for those who seek to escape conquest and tyranny, is the one who breaks his vow. The one who is a soldier in time of war, killing that he must take life in the cause of that which is right and true, and who understands what he is doing, is prepared that his human nature in this incarnation, and in later ones, shall suffer that bad *karma* which results from the deed of taking life. He makes this sacrifice under the guidance of love and compassion, for the sake of his family and nation, the two wonderful units created by the Planetary Spirit to make his home on the earth, and cause his first duties and his first experiences.

Of course I am not speaking of conscripts. The *karma* of men born into a nation where conscription is the law must evidently be a heavy one. Some of them go to battle in the true spirit of devotion, and clearly, if they are disciples, the motive for their action changes the nature of the action, and they do not break their vow. But those who go unwillingly are surely expiating past offences against the divine law, and are being hastened over the long path of unconscious evolution.

I have become aware in the ethereal world of these two types of soldiers of my country, where I have seen voluntary service give place to conscription because so many were unawakened to their national duty.

In January 1916 I was taken with others to witness a very curious and unexpected thing. We went into a large and very beautiful garden, where we found Lord Kitchener, quite alone. He was standing on the grass under a great tree; I and those I was with remained some distance away on the grass. I discovered then that there were spokesmen among us ; one after another went out from the group, approached him, and made a speech. The tenor of all these speeches was that of admiration, of absolute confidence in him, of encouragement because of great trouble and difficulty which he must experience later on ; the last speaker spoke of an ordeal, and of purification. He received these messages of confidence and friendship with apparent pleasure, but he was very pale and he looked very sad. I saw that he wore his Field-Marshal's uniform, but it was white, with gold facings and decorations. When all was over, he went away first, going up a steep ascent, so that he was soon much higher up than we were. My impression was that he must be in immediate danger, either of illness or death, and I watched anxiously to see what might happen. Not till June did the blow fall.

I relate this only because of the white uniform. I did not understand it till I was taken to see a muster in the ethereal world of the New Army who have fallen in the battlefield. All wore white, that pure white which is worn by those who have fulfilled the Law. The uniform is identical with that worn by the soldier in his physical life, but it is white for those who responded to the call. The conscript's ethereal uniform is black— the colour of earthly desires, of love of physical life, of worldly ambitions. The men who have only gone at the long last, unwillingly, because they were building up businesses, amassing fortunes, or enjoying the spending of them, show this when they emerge into the higher fields by wearing the uniform of darkness. They have died un- willing deaths, and their souls hunger for material life and prosperity. The unwilling- ness to die, or to lose those we love by death, attracts the darkness, and this interior fact is the real origin of the wearing of mourning in the form of black clothes. If death were re- garded as the gateway to life, as the ancient Egyptians taught in the miscalled *Book of the Dead* (which should be called the Book of the Living), the wearing of mourning would disappear naturally.

The double nature of the threefold injunc- tions gives rise to a paradox which is like a contradiction. The disciple who has con- quered ambition yet works as arduously and unceasingly for the helping of the world and the urging on of evolution as the ambitious man works for his own ends. And none respect life so deeply as those do who no longer desire it, for they have begun to guess at its mystery and would not willingly deprive the smallest insect of life breathed into it by the divine, which alone can give and maintain this priceless gift.

The disciple seeks no happiness or comfort on the two lower of the fivefold fields, for he knows that no pleasure thus obtained is permanent. He seeks to open out into the state of pure bliss which cannot be disturbed ; and that effort in itself makes him happy as those are who live for happiness, though he be deprived of all external conditions of pleasure or of comfort.

CHAPTER II

WORK AND EFFORT—SEPARATENESS— SENSATION

" Work as those work who are ambitious."

THERE is a great teaching in this apparently simple rule. Work is of many different orders. No such work is done by any other class of workers as by those who are ambitious. It has in it the quality of effort. The ambitious man is always aiming at an improved position; he is always trying to rise, and therefore the most mechanical and arduous toil, if undertaken by him, is changed in its nature to something full of dreams and glory. A mechanic who works arduously, determined to become a master, may labour unceasingly at a monotonous task, and yet the whole of the work will be tinged by the quality which brings success.

The determination to work as those work who are ambitious must dominate the aspirations of the spirit during the interval between the incarnations, in order that the coming life on earth shall have the power of rising upward by effort without the stimulus of personal ambition. Such lives are of the greatest value to the world, the stir of their uprising waking the sleeping souls about them. It is like the fluttering of an angel's wings, waking man to a sense of wonder as to its purpose.

"KILL OUT ALL SENSE OF SEPARATION"

The sense of separateness is known in some schools of occultism as the great heresy. It is known in all schools to mean separateness from the Supreme.

The disciple who has recognised the divine spark within himself can undertake the task of killing out the sense of separateness with some hope of success. But even for him it is a difficult task and a severe one. That firmament which the Creating Spirit placed in the heavens seems to man to separate him from God, who, he imagines, dwells above and beyond it. To some it seems like the shell of an egg within which the spirit of the race is sown as a seed, and germinates in the mystic darkness, while God and His light are without it, all round it. A very ancient teaching is that the stars are that same great light shining through little openings. Such ideas show how in the mind of man matter and the divine are entirely different and are separated by a great gulf.

The teaching of *Light on the Path* is that no such separateness exists, and that the sense of it is a delusion born of darkness and ignorance. Like all those which form and surround human life, this delusion is necessary for the development of the human spirit. That spirit is bidden to stand alone—away from the Supreme, so that it may gaze upon Him. The "isolation of the soul," a mystic condition spoken of by Patanjali, is thus reached by the advanced Yogin. Individuality becomes a possession of the ego which constantly increases in power and perfection, by reason of this isolation. No help or aid on the way comes save from the Eternal; man, even the man himself, is but a seed hidden in the darkness from which the flower of disciplehood must spring up. And these flowers arise separately, isolated, each on its slender stem. But the Ray passes into each, and into the very seed itself, into the darkness, so that there is no separateness. With-

out that Ray man could not be. The stem
which supports him, slender as it seems, is
strong as life itself, and the disciple, who is
growing as the flower grows, is never apart
from the Supreme on which he gazes, and
therefore for him "all manner of thing shall
be well."

"KILL OUT DESIRE FOR SENSATION"

The ego which seeks rebirth under the
ordinary conditions of humanity, desires to
return to human life, for the very purpose of
obtaining sensation. The passional nature
of the man dwelling on the astral plane
draws his spirit back towards the earth, which
is, for it, the place of fulfilment and gratifica-
tion. The disciple who recognises that this
is the power of the darkness drawing him
away from the light will endeavour throughout the interval between the incarnations to
preserve the equipoise which he has attained.
If he can stand firmly in the presence of the
Master of the Eon, he will enter upon rebirth for training, for development, and not
for the sake of sensation. Then he will be
able to be a helper of the world. Sensation
overwhelms the whole being, like a great
tide, and the submerged spirit has to be

bathed in it before it is possible to emerge from it. Sometimes the desire for it is so strong that it is necessary to go through the experience, the ungratified longing being an obstacle in the Path. Genius is often a manifestation of this state, and that is why great artists and poets and musicians are so wise and are found to know so much. They are disciples who have come to earth to gratify the passion for beauty, and to experience a whole incarnation drenched in the sensation of it.

This obstacle arises again when it has been conquered on this field of experience. The ethereal world is full of such transcendent beauty, the being who dwells in it experiences such keen joy of life, that Patanjali speaks of it as holding greater dangers than does earth life. The highly developed being, whose glorious home is in that world, may be called upon by his Higher Self to rebirth in the physical world as an awakening and an expiation. Tempted by the delights of a life inconceivable to the imagination of man, he longs to remain there amid the exquisite beauty of it, and loses the impetus to rise into the spiritual world beyond. Then that resonant voice which is the silence itself will

6

arise, and call upon him to look for the Warrior and return to the battle.

KILL OUT THE HUNGER FOR GROWTH

As sensation reappears to become an obstacle in the path, to the disciple who has gone a great distance upon it, so does ambition spring up once more and become a great danger in its subtle and hidden shape. The ambition of man, which raises him from the state of the sluggard, is as a tiny weed on an arid, wind-blown northern hillside, compared to that which arises in the heart of the disciple—a giant weed, a tropical growth. The hunger to become absolutely purified, to become truly great, to rise above the stature of man, creates the ordeal which may come at the first step of the " perilous ladder "—or the last. Again must the heart be made to bleed by the drawing out from it of roots which have become a part of its very structure. The disciple has to grow as the flower grows, *unconsciously*, his attention altogether removed from himself and riveted upon the Supreme.

POWER—PEACE—POSSESSIONS

Having conquered ambition, the disciple is told to desire power ; having voluntarily entered the battle, he is told to desire peace; having conquered the desires for life and for sensation, he is told to desire possessions. This is the great paradox of occultism, arising from the state of crucifixion. He has to transmute the obstacles within himself to aids upon the path.

The six desires are really three, presented in their twofold aspect. The clue to the paradox is found in the first sentence of Rule 16 : " Those possessions must belong to the pure soul only, and be possessed therefore by all pure souls equally."

The disciple is told to desire only that which is within him ; for within him is the light of the world—the Christos. And in this highest nature of man is that power which shall make him appear nothing in the eyes of men, but which shall raise him to the Supreme.

He is told to desire only that which is beyond him ; and yet to desire peace fervently. Peace is beyond him, for he is still in the battle. No peace can be obtained in the three lower fields of evolution by the disciple, for he works as those work who are ambitious, and his ceaseless effort is to rise. He is told to desire only that which is unattainable, and to desire possessions above all.

Those possessions are the especial property of the whole only when united, and are therefore only to be obtained when the race is ready to go forth at the great gate of liberation, and to enter as a whole into freedom and light.

CHAPTER III

THE RETREAT—THE ADVANCE—THE BLOOMING OF THE FLOWER

THE disciple is bidden himself to seek out the way. He does not wait to be guided or to be shown it ; he does not look for indications and hesitate unless they are forthcoming ; he knows that he intends to find the way, and his search for it is ceaseless and unwavering. All else must give place to it. And yet all else is duly served and attended to because he knows that he may not overlook or neglect anything whatever. The ordinary man may pass things by, and regard them as being of no concern to him. Not so the disciple. Whatever comes in his path, whether painful or pleasant, is for him ; for he has to know all and to experience all. But ever present with him is the paramount duty, the task which stands above all others, of finding the *Way*.

And what is this way?

"Whither I go ye know, and the Way ye know."

Is it not manifestly the ascent from being to being, from world to world? From the lowest of the fivefold fields to the highest? Is not that indeed the climbing of the "perilous ladder"? Is not that indeed the rising from the tomb of matter, into which the Christ descended and from which He rose again, into which the Christos of every man descends, to rise again in due time?

The retreating within, the giving of attention to the constitution of one's own inner being, reveals the amazing fact that the spark of the Divine is there; though it may be the merest speck of light engulfed in darksome clouds, submerged in matter. But it is within; it is there. It is nowhere else to be found, until that spark shall have suddenly become a conscious light and know itself as a being with power to withdraw into the occult hidden states and take form and live in those states. But the soul must know the divine which is in itself to be the divine and naught else. It must contemplate it and recognise it and perform the profound obeisance, knowing itself to be God. From that hour the man knows himself to be sacred, and to be indeed the temple of the living God. Life takes on a new meaning, a new vitality, a new reality.

Now is it possible to make the advance into outer life with the boldness of perfect confidence. The disciple knows with certainty now that no mistake can be made. There is no such thing as a mistake, any more than there can be an accident. All is ordered, all is foreseen, all is known. When men fling themselves into the bottomless pit of evil, protecting angels watch over them and follow them into the depths. The disciple cannot grow in limitation; he must know all life, experience all trial and all joy. The man's *karma* places him in positions of testing and difficulty of all kinds from incarnation to incarnation. All human life must be known to him before rebirth is ended. The disciple which arises within him enables him to look upward with the eyes of the flower out from the darkness of earth; so soon as it opens it blooms into the glory of the spiritual light. The stem will be guarded and cared for by the Gardener, and no stress of joy or pain, no storms of emotion, will break or bend it. The man and the disciple are alike fearless, knowing all is well; and the ego advances into outer life boldly, taking great strides, doing strong actions, influencing the men about him, colouring the atmosphere that surrounds him. By these signs it may be guessed that the flower has bloomed. Its beauty is seen from above, but its fragrance pours forth on all sides and makes life a better thing for all who are near it, even on the lowest of the fivefold fields.

CHAPTER IV

CONTEMPLATION—THE STUDY OF MAN-KIND—THE STUDY OF THE SELF—THE LOGOS

THE state attained by the conquest of the lower mind and senses, from which a power of discernment arises, is developed by stages. It cannot be hastened, because it is consequent upon, and dependent upon, the five vows being absolutely fulfilled and confirmed. As the nature becomes purified by the unceasing adherence to these vows, so the hearing or power of discernment opens out. Contemplation, which is the first step in this development, is defined by Patanjali as the fixing of the mind upon something. The unity of the mind with that which it contemplates is called absorption ; this is followed by the mystic trance, and the three together cause a state in which all is known to the Yogin. He has attained to omniscience in respect to all created objects. The wonderful knowledge which comes to him is a temptation which arises at the last step of the "perilous ladder." He may be so completely absorbed as to remain in the trance of knowledge and perception for an Eon unless roused by the Warrior within him. He is beyond the temptations of the ethereal world where subtle sensation might have delayed him on the way; he is intoxicated with the wine of pure knowledge and perception. There is a later state of contemplation when the mind becomes "deflected towards discrimination" and "bowed down to isolation." It is in fact conquered, and no effort has any longer to be made to reach these states or retain them. After this arises the constant flow of pure discrimination. The state of meditation without a seed has been reached. The object is contemplated without the interference of any previous thought in the mind, and no thought arises in consequence of absorption in the object contemplated. The mind has become simply a transparent jewel which reflects the object contemplated. When the disciple is told to regard earnestly the life that surrounds him, he is understood to have attained to the power of contemplation as practised by the Yogins, and to be capable of entering into the nature of all the different kinds of life which support and surround the human race in the fivefold fields, the animals and fish and birds, the animalculæ, the countless organisms with which nature teems, surround the human race on the physical plane. Their astral forms surround him in the astral world; but there appear there also many other forms of life— elemental beings, usually inimical to man, and other beings of which we are only conscious when acting and living in that world. There are beings which correspond in position to animals in this world, but which are not their astral forms, for they never descend into the lowest field. They are met with sometimes in dream-consciousness; the drug-takers and drunkards are familiar with them. In the ethereal world man is surrounded by most friendly beings who aid and help him voluntarily, and do that which he needs, at the dictation of those who are guarding and guiding him. Sometimes these take animal or birdlike forms— there are most beautiful horses who know more than their riders and can be trusted to carry them safely and to guard them from danger.   I have seen these beings in great herds, waiting to help men who in their ethereal forms are not yet able to move freely or accomplish great distances.   I have seen one who carried a Master of the Order of Love from one interior world to another, and also carried his messages for him.   I know of a wonderful birdlike form which does not belong to any species of earthly birds, and which is the manifestation in that world of a most gentle and kind being—not in any sense human, yet beneficently friendly to man.   I have been placed like a child on his broad back, and have nestled safely into the blue-green feathers as into a down bed, while his great wings spread out and he carried me from world to world, through the interstellar spaces.   Higher still, on the verge of the spiritual state are the angels, and the archangels, and the Forces personified which makes the phenomenal world the wonderful thing it is.   And none of these beings are in the same school as man, none of them are on his wheel of evolution.   They follow entirely different laws, their moral code is entirely different, what their goal is we know not, nor are we told to try and discover.   But all that lives, whether small or large, near or distant, are we told to contemplate and to regard earnestly. By so doing we shall obtain knowledge of its nature and its properties.

It must be noted that to look into the hearts of men is to come later than the study of the surrounding life. The power of intelligence is needed before it is possible to truly comprehend our fellow-men, even those nearest and dearest to us. Yet they have to be understood before the end of the pilgrimage. This can only be attempted, it is only permitted, when the disciple is able to look past the action to the motive, and when he can view both motive and action impersonally, and without judgment. Our Master said, "Judge not." This was not said to ordinary men, but to His disciples. A disciple may not, and cannot, judge any other whether upon the long way of ordinary life, or the shortened way of occultism. In order to look intelligently into the hearts of men he must not only have conquered himself but must have cleared away all mists from his eyes. He must be able to gaze upon a human heart as the Brothers of Love gaze upon it, without any personal human feeling arising to confuse the vision. It is necessary that he should look upon the hearts of men in order that he shall know that race of which he is a part. And although all men take all steps, yet every man is individualised, and therefore each man takes each step differently. It means a separate thing for him from what it means to any other; it is a unique experience in every single instance. And the disciple has to become omniscient and to know men as he knows all else.

REGARD MOST EARNESTLY YOUR OWN HEART

Why this rule comes so late, near the end of the second set of rules which can be undertaken only by the highly advanced Yogin, is that it can only be carried out by one who has entirely conquered personality, and is able to gaze upon himself as impartially as upon any other. This point at which his own heart can be contemplated is one to look towards from the very commencement of the whole effort, because it is through the understanding of that marvellous organ of emotion that the one light comes which can illuminate life and make it clear to the seer who gazes upon it. The hidden mysteries of the phenomenal universe can be understood by means of contemplation, separately, but that transcendent mystery called *life* can only be seen with knowledge by one who has attained the power of gazing upon himself, and seeing all things in the light of the Ray within him. That Ray emanates from the Logos, and the disciple who can perceive it in his own heart, and by its light look upon the hearts of other men, and upon the "constantly changing moving life formed by the hearts of men," is ready for *Speech*. Not until then is he ready; for it is written, "*Speech comes only with knowledge.*"

I have said in the chapter on "Speech," "When the actions are of such a nature that they become manifested in the ethereal and spiritual worlds then the Masters perceive them." This point now reached in the development of the disciple is that at which this takes place. No actions which are done in the physical world are manifested in the ethereal and spiritual worlds until the disciple has attained this power of perceiving all life through the Ray in his own heart. Then he is capable of deeds which are not only great but entirely impersonal. Seen by the light of the Ray the life of the all is the life of the man himself. He does not act from outside like the philanthropist with riches who gives a dole to the poor man, leaving him poor, while he remains rich. He is all men as well as himself, and every action is done for all, himself being one of the all. The Logos thus enters into all men, and when the disciple attains to that mode of action he is with and in the Logos itself. That joy then comes to him of being drawn up in the Ray to the Great Heart from which it emanates, there to find himself within all knowledge and all light, absolutely at home.

CHAPTER V

THE GIFTS OF THE DISCIPLE—THE USE OF THE GIFTS—THE VICTORY

THAT state of contemplation which is called the mystic trance, because the seer is unconscious of himself, being conscious only of the object he gazes upon, brings to him all occult powers. He is able to understand moments and their order, and is no longer impeded by the delusion of time. By the contemplations of the relationship between the body he is using, and the ether, he obtains release from the law of gravitation, and loses the impediment of weight, so that he can soar through space and walk upon air or water. By gazing upon the air and acquiring the knowledge of its quality, he becomes self-illuminating and can shed a blazing light around him should he desire to do so. He can enter into another body and use its powers, the laws of bondage being relaxed for him as a consequence of his power

7

of obtaining knowledge.   He can use the strength of an elephant, or the wings of a bird, or the microscopic sight of an insect. These are lent to him willingly because his approach to the beings whose powers he desires to use is in the spirit of non-*himsâ* (non-killing), or absolute love and compassion.   He can enter into any object of sense, whether minute, concealed, or distant, and obtain that intimacy with it which is all but the same as being itself.   A speck of sand on the seashore reveals all its life and beauty to him.   The stars and their courses show themselves to him.   He has admission to the starry regions, and the road above the horizon, and learns those things which the ancient Egyptians knew to be taught to all men after death.   He conquers death, and rises to those states which to ordinary men are only open after the physical body is laid aside.   There is indeed for him no death, as he dwells and moves in all the fivefold fields, with more or less power and strength according to the perfection of his development.   He has the friendship and love of all men, for he has but to regard them with his compassionate nature and they are drawn towards him as by a magnet.   He has the

THE GIFTS OF THE DISCIPLE

same power with all whom he encounters in
the space between the earth and the sun,
which is thickly peopled with friends and foes
of the ordinary man, and in the starry regions,
and all the fivefold fields. All beings love
him. He has knowledge of the past and
future; he can look into his past incarnations; he can affect the character of coming
incarnations, changing his rank on rebirth,
and obtaining a pure and perfect body. He
can make the body he is occupying invisible;
he can cause cessation of hunger and thirst in
himself; he can understand the language of
all created beings, even of the insects of the
earth, and of the angels of heaven; he can
obtain knowledge of the mutability of forms,
and the structure of bodies. The Powers
invite him to witness marvellous spectacles,
and to perceive the pageants of nature and
supernature. Patanjali warns the Yogin
that there must be neither pleasure nor pride
arising in the heart of the disciple in consequence of these invitations from Powers and
Angelic Beings. He is still only a student,
and the black magician can obtain these gifts
and receive these invitations in the same
degree as the disciple. It is now that "great
ones fall back from the threshold." A

terrible warning is given at the end of the
second set of rules. Your knowledge is
described then as a trust vested in you by the
Most High. " Betray it, misuse your knowledge, or neglect it," and you may fall from
the place you have reached, to the very foot
of the ladder. The knowledge you have is
part of the wealth of the united spirit of life.
It must be used for the all, not in any sense
for the man himself, or for any beloved whom
he loves more than himself. And the man
himself alone can know his motives and judge
whether he is selfish or unselfish. He is the
judge of his own actions as he is the arbiter
of his own destiny. Though he is surrounded
in earth and heaven by wise friends, by
helpers, guides, yet he is his own guide and
friend in the great realities, for none else
truly knows him. The Osiris who is his
judge is the Osiris within him; he himself
holds the scales.

Now when he has reached the summit the
hour is reached when he must regard most
earnestly his own heart and look into his
own being. It is only by keeping his attention on the divine spark within him that he
can find any help. The uses to which his
gifts are put are the constant test to the

disciple of his condition and motive. When he has conquered all desire for possessions save those which can be possessed by all pure souls equally, then he can command all wealth. In the quaint language of the Yoga aphorisms "All jewels approach him." He has but to put out his hand and it is filled. No longer does necessity or difficulty impede him. But now is the crucial test of his true direction, in the use he makes of the phenomenal world and its treasures, which have become his own and with which he can do what he will. And what is it that he wills? It is in his power without difficulty and without effort to take the stones from a diamond mine, or the hidden gold from mountain fastnesses, and scatter these treasures among the poor of the great cities. He will not do this, for he is under the Great Master of the Eon, who said, " The poor ye have always with you." Poverty is one of those lessons prepared with the utmost care for the spirits of men, for the development of those who need that limitation. The disciple may move amongst these men and aid them to learn their lesson, and give help to those on whom the lesson may be bearing too hardly ; but he will not interfere with the lesson itself which he knows is God-sent. There is enough gold in the world for all men to be rich, but it is certain that forces directed by the *karmas* of men lead it into certain channels and away from others. And so with all sources of comfort or pleasure.

What, then, are the uses of the gifts of the disciple? They are interior and follow occult laws. As men begin to rise above their fellows and look upwards, springing from the earth in which they have been buried, they need help; it comes to them, on the physical plane, often most mysteriously. To the Masters it is known that among the friends of such a one is a disciple who can bring new associations from the other side of the world if it is required, without difficulty. This lowest fivefold field is really as full of mystery as any of the others, and it is intimately associated with those above it. Darkness, hopelessness, lack of life and opportunity exist only for those who turn away from the light and refuse to look upon the Ray within.

The Brotherhood of Love knows all that takes place on earth and directs the disciple in the use of his gifts. In this world of matter he is practically omnipotent and can do all things. But what he does is done under the mystic rule and law of the Christ. Let no man think himself alone or without help even on the very lowest rung of the ladder. Though he may not yet have begun to aspire to grow upward, he is carefully watched and guarded, and the gifts of the disciple are used for him, to bring light into his darkness, so soon as he looks for light.

THE VICTORY

The Bhagavad Gîtâ states that by performing actions people conquer perishable worlds—but that the man of understanding attains by knowledge to the everlasting glory—for there is no other way to it. The knowable has then become small, as Patanjali expresses it at the end of the Yoga aphorisms, and the soul being centred in itself has attained to Isolation. Death is swallowed up in Victory, for the ego has risen above rebirth and has conquered himself so that he can stand unfalteringly in the presence of the Masters. He can stand before them all now, the Great Ones of all time, who regard him as one near at hand, no longer in a far country.

But the gate of freedom is not open yet, for the veil has to be lifted which is spread over all nations. We shall all be changed; we must all be changed; Victory is for the race, and the disciple who has conquered, and is ready to pass out into the glory, becomes the humble servant of those who have not yet begun to look for the light, seeking to aid them to find the way. "Many shall be purified and made white, and tried—none of the wicked shall understand; but the wise shall understand." This understanding is a gift of the disciple, always to be used for the service of the many who lag behind in the great pilgrimage. Now is he greatly tried—his strength is tested to the uttermost. He is still upon the battlefield of the race, urging men to pass beyond it and reach towards the glory. And he has himself to hold to that which has no substance, to listen to the silence, and to gaze on the invisible. He no longer gazes on "the Sight"; he no longer hears the song of life. Yet wrapped in the ecstasy of the unseen vision and the soundless voice, he walks the earth unrecognised by men, having conquered—one who is victorious.

EPILOGUE

"I AND MY FATHER"

THE stanzas of *Light on the Path* are written for all time, and therefore "the Masters" are spoken of without distinction. The same rules are given to all disciples whatever the period of evolution. From the earliest till now, and till the end, throughout the three times, the way is the same. But with the movement of the great wheel of evolution the Masters who help and serve the race change. Pure and glorious spirits controlled the development of prehistoric Egypt, which created art and civilisation for the world, and they will return again to help disciples when "in the distance of time" Egypt again rises as the true leader of the nations. Over these Masters and those who have taken their places throughout different periods of the world's history reign the Avatars, the Great Ones. These follow a mystic law higher than any we can conceive of in human terms of thought. This present period is the deepest point of the dread pilgrimage through matter; the wheel of evolution has reached a depth in its rotations from which it must, sooner or later, turn upward.

At no other point would the great world-war have been possible. The darkness and evil, the passional nature of man, is at its strongest, and is striving to submerge the whole race and draw it down, so that, as it would be expressed in ordinary human language, it would be lost for ever. Occult-ists know that this apparent eternity is the stupendous length of an æon, and that then, with bad Karma to work out in physical life, the race would be struggling to begin over again, crippled, diseased, all but disin-tegrated. This will not be, because of the law of the pains of opposites, because of the power of crucifixion. With the darkness combats the light; and into the darkest being the Ray enters. The white-robed rise into the ethereal plane from the battle-field and the hospital, and the desolated homes, having fulfilled the Law, and obeyed the call of duty. Because this is the darkest hour of the race, because the wheel is at the lowest turn, because man is being tested in the fire of hate and horror, the highest and most perfect of the *Avatars* known to the world is in charge of it. The cosmic spirit of the Christ descended from that state in which He dwelled with the Supreme, and came right down into matter, so that He should bear the burden of the Cross with man right through the Eon. He knows all man's frailty, and all man's temptations, having made Himself a son of man. But He is One with His Father, gazing always on the Supreme, so that from the highest place help comes to every man—intimate, loving help—even if he is in danger of falling into the bottomless pit. And many, how many we cannot guess, are drawn back from that danger by the Good Shepherd who seeks the lost sheep—and there is joy in heaven over the repentant sinner.

To make plainer what I am trying to express I will quote from the Prologue of *As the Flower Grows* what I wrote there of the Great Master's work for us at this present time:

"Some part of what I have seen myself on the battlefield of 1914–1915 I will set forth as plainly as possible; for it deeply concerns my theme, and bears on it.

"One figure which is always present in the thick of the battle, and has been since the first shots were fired, is one which holds no rank in any of the armies, yet it is there on that blood-drenched ground, where none but combatants may be, amongst the men, beside the officers, with and close to everyone who is concerned in the war. This sounds as though it were omnipresent, and so it is. The ordinary physical does not perceive this Presence, and therefore to the soldier who has not yet suffered it is not visible. But extreme agony dulls the physical sight and opens the inner eyes. The figure which stands beside the wounded soldier seems as a vision, and may only be remembered as a dream is; but for the moment its intense reality overpowers all else. The horror of the war fades, the dreadful emotions aroused by it disappear from the heart, and even the agony of the physical wound is blurred. The Presence alone does all this; the pain is worth enduring for the sake of this amazing experience of actual acquaintance with the healer of men.

"The *Avatar*, who is now the Great Master of the world, who came straight from God to man, and kept the Way open from man to God for all who will follow in His steps, promised to stay with us to the end of the Eon, and to become visible again to man, in the ethereal world. 'All who suffer so deeply that the bonds of the physical relax their hold, know that this promise is kept.'

"The Christ lives and moves on the inner or higher planes of being, passing to and fro, and taking on different forms according to which world He is in. The long battle front is terrible on the physical plane, more terrible still upon the astral plane, and reveals an awful and amazing beauty on the ethereal plane.

"Upon the astral plane at the very first I saw Him hanging on the Cross, bleeding from the nails through His hands and feet— the form which His Presence takes wherever sin and hatred are stronger than the spirit of love in the hearts of men. This Form hovered over the firing line, like a crucifix carried on high, unutterable sadness on the Face."

Because of its meaning, and the reality of the symbol, in the French villages it seemed as though no bombardment could destroy the crucifix. The photograph taken of the one at Neuve Chapelle, standing intact amid the ruined houses, is familiar to everyone. An officer who was near there soon after saw the same thing in neighbouring villages, and he told me that he heard the men frequently remark upon the strangeness of the circumstance. In one place I have heard about, the Cross itself fell, but the figure lay upon the ground uninjured. The crucifix at Misery was photographed by the Canadian war photographer, standing intact above the absolutely wrecked village.

I want now to pass to another aspect which He wears in the astral world, and I will again quote from *As the Flower Grows*, in which I describe these aspects:

"From the astral world it is possible to look upon the physical world (it is on the ethereal plane that physical bodies fade from view altogether). Therefore I was able to see the heaped bodies of the dead, and to perceive that some were not quite dead, and to pause and think how great the suffering must be. And then suddenly I saw moving amongst the bodies the Glorious Presence as the Good Shepherd carrying His lanterns. He was stooping over the dead, looking closely upon them, searching among them. Now and again He bent closer and seemed to draw something upwards. And I saw then that He was releasing souls not strong enough to release themselves, and I understood that He was gathering in His flock. He passed across the line. I saw Him move hither and thither on both sides, seeking His own from either field, from both opponents, from all armies."

Later on in the progress of the war I became aware of Him in a third aspect, one which I had never yet seen. " He was not on the Cross, yet His wounds bled; and they were not the wounds in His hands and feet. He was covered with wounds, and His white feet were stained with the blood that fell upon them. And He cried aloud, 'Verily I say unto you, inasmuch as ye did it unto one of these My brethren, unto one of these least, ye did it unto Me.' This dreadful scene I saw enacted and re-enacted night after night for weeks. I learned then that the Christ indeed suffers with the humanity He loves; He serves and suffers. When I awoke it was with the consciousness that I had been kneeling at those bloodstained feet. I saw this so often, I suppose, because there was so much to learn about it. One thing I learned I can now set down, and that was that these innocents whose wounds were inflicted upon the suffer-

ing Christ were not only children slain in
cold blood for sheer cruelty; many were
young soldiers who felt no longing for
battle, who scarcely understood for what
they suffered and died.

"So far I have spoken of what I have seen
on the astral plane, that next to the physical,
where the suffering and the horror are as
great and indeed much greater than on the
physical plane. The Christ is visible to all,
the crucified and suffering Christ.

"After a long time of witnessing these
terrible scenes I was one night, quite unex-
pectedly and suddenly, led on to the ethereal
plane. My guide left me, and I was a little
child standing alone, awestruck. I knew I
was in the trenches, and in the whole length
of them, the miles and miles of them, grew
tall, white Madonna lilies. Oh, the lilies!
the sight and the scent of the lilies, the
glorious blooms, the overpowering fragrance!
Where souls pass through death to spiritual
glory, the great white lily springs up at the
passing, and makes the quivering ether sweet.
I looked afar and saw in the dim distance
the line of the white flowers. And this was
the terrible firing line!—a garden such as
has never before been seen. Suddenly I be-

came aware of a quiet figure approaching me noiselessly, moving through the tall flowers. It was the Christ as the Good Shepherd. He looked from right to left down among the flowers, and I knew that He was looking to see if any lost sheep had been left behind, and needed Him. And I knew that He had thus slowly paced the whole great length of the firing line, peacefully, quietly.

"For many days and nights I was here among the lilies—then I was taken suddenly straight to the spiritual world. I was still among the flowers. I still saw the long line of lilies going into the distance each way. But from where I stood—where a bitter battle had just been fought on the physical plane, and terrible results from it were being tended on the astral plane—from where I stood, a spirit in the spiritual world, I saw a great wide avenue in front, going uphill. The avenue was formed of magnolia trees in full bloom, the glorious ethereal counterparts of the magnolia tree of ancient Egypt.

"The Christ was passing up the avenue, and I knew that He had helped many, many souls to go up that way during the last few hours of horror in the physical world. He had returned from one of His searches

8

among the lilies. He carried in His arms one who was asleep, who was too tired and worn to awake into the spiritual world to which he had earned the right of entrance. I was able to follow Him, though with difficulty—helped mysteriously to do so. A great dome of white marble was visible at the summit of the hill; white marble steps led up to a wide, open door. The Christ passed up the steps carrying His burden. I followed Him, afraid, yet not afraid, for I knew I was permitted, or I could not have been there. Within the doors I saw the soft, shining waters of a great pool, like an indoor lake so large was it; and I knew that the running water which passed through, and gently disturbed it, was the Water of Life. Many lay there, upheld by the mystic water, growing young and whole again. The Christ gave His sleeping charge into the care of this water, laying the form gently upon it. The little movement of the water was like the movement of a cradle, and I saw a faint smile on the tired face, and then a deeper sleep, full of profound healing, enwrap the weary consciousness. The Christ walked across the water to the other side, I following Him, but I think I was carried.

Then I gazed upon that which I cannot describe. Words are useless. A vast temple, full of light — roofless. The rays of the Logos poured down from above. Spirits sprang from the water, wakening full of strength, unknowing of the weariness left behind, and each was drawn to its own Ray and became as a flame, and was drawn up into it."

"In my Father's house are many mansions," said the Master. One I have now seen myself, and it proves to me more plainly even than the experiences of the wondrous day when I saw[1] the glorious writing ("Light on the Path") on the wall, that now it is before the Christ those who are disciples must be strong enough to stand with the feet washed in the blood of the heart. I have seen Him with His feet stained with His own heart's blood, and only so can we present ourselves before Him in His own likeness.

[1] See, for the description of this, *When the Sun Moves Northward*, chap. x.

Printed in the USA
CPSIA information can be obtained
at www.ICGtesting.com
LVHW070237090124
768362LV00021B/1474